ROADRUNNERS

RIO NUEVO PUBLISHERS®
P.O. Box 5250, Tucson, Arizona 85703-0250
(520) 623-9558, www.rionuevo.com

Design: Karen Schober, Seattle, Washington

Library of Congress Cataloging-in-Publication Data

Kaufman, Lynn Hassler.
Roadrunners / Lynn Hassler Kaufman.
     p. cm. -- (Look West series)
ISBN-13: 978-1-887896-64-1 ; ISBN-10: 1-887896-64-3 (cloth)
1. Roadrunner. I. Title. II. Series: Look West.
QL696.C83K38 2005
598.7'4--dc22

                              2004016595

Printed in China
10 9 8 7 6 5 4 3 2

ROADRUNNERS

Lynn Hassler Kaufman

LOOK WEST
SERIES

RIO NUEVO PUBLISHERS
TUCSON, ARIZONA

A CURIOUS-LOOKING BIRD WITH A ROGUISH AIR
AND SHAGGY CREST TROTS ACROSS THE ROAD AND MAKES OFF
INTO THE BRUSH. AT A SAFE DISTANCE FROM THE PAVEMENT, IT
PAUSES AND LOOKS ABOUT, ELEVATING THE FEATHERS OF ITS FLOPPY
CREST AND BRINGING ITS LONG TAIL SLOWLY UPWARD. SUDDENLY
THE BIRD FREEZES AT ATTENTION. A FAST-MOVING WHIPTAIL LIZARD
APPEARS FROM BEHIND A CACTUS, SPOTS THE LARGE BIRD, AND
MAKES HASTE IN THE OPPOSITE DIRECTION. BOTH ANIMALS DASH
OFF AND DISAPPEAR BEHIND A THICKET. MOMENTS LATER,
THE BIRD SAUNTERS OUT WITH THE END OF THE
LIZARD'S TAIL HANGING OUT OF ITS MOUTH.

This is the notorious roadrunner, the state bird of New Mexico and one of the most famous birds of the American Southwest. In the public's imagination, roadrunners are among the most fictionalized of birds. Members of some generations may think of them as oddly shaped, purple cartoon characters that run down roads, occasionally stopping to utter a rather annoying "beep beep." Others may conjure up memories of a popular automobile of the late 1960s and early 1970s. Regarded by many as a symbol of magic and good luck, the real bird, known as the greater roadrunner by birdwatchers and ornithologists, may seem somewhat anticlimactic when actually observed. Streaky and brown with very long tails, roadrunners are rather strange and unearthly looking. They don't outrun cars or go "beep beep"; but start paying close attention to their lifestyles, and we discover that they are impressive and fascinating creatures.

Roadrunners are elusive birds, generally found singly or in pairs, and are mostly silent. Although they can fly, they seem reluctant to do so, instead preferring to spend most of their time walking briskly on the ground. With short, rounded wings, they lack the ability to fly long distances. Instead, they have powerful legs well adapted for running and capable of sprinting at speeds up to fifteen

ABOVE: A 1968 Plymouth Roadrunner.   RIGHT: A roadrunner wrestles with a snake.

miles per hour. They don't just speed about for fun; these effective predators use their swiftness to capture fast-moving insects and lizards.

Even more enthralling than seeing them run and hunt is watching
their alluring courtship display. Males bow and prance, wag their tails, and
offer nesting material and food to their intended mates.

‖ EVERYBODY'S FAVORITE CUCKOO ‖

After watching the antics of these zany-looking birds, it seems fitting that they are classified as members of the cuckoo family, or Cuculidae. The word "cuckoo" may be synonymous with "crazy," but these

birds have a bad reputation for other reasons as well. The family group as a whole is notorious for the fact that some species lay their eggs in other birds' nests and use foster parents to raise their young. The common cuckoo of Europe (whose voice is imitated by the cuckoo clock) is the most infamous in this regard. The word "cuckold" comes from the word "cuckoo" and is used to designate a husband whose wife has wandered afield, just as these female birds do.

Members of the cuckoo family found in North America generally raise their own young. Representatives include the anis, odd-looking, gregarious, all-black birds found in tropical areas; the black-billed and yellow-billed cuckoos, which live in trees and occasionally use other birds to raise their young; and the ground-dwelling roadrunners, among the largest and most distinctive members of the group. Unlike some of their cousins, roadrunners are responsible parents, building their own nests and bringing up their own young. Much more predatory than any of their relatives, roadrunners will tackle just about anything they run across.

Like other cuckoos, the roadrunner is a zygodactyl bird, which means that it has two toes that point forward and two that point backward. The X-shaped feet allow for great flexibility and extensibility on flat surfaces, facilitating what the bird does best: walking and running. Clawed feet also enable the birds to climb adroitly from limb to limb in trees or shrubs.

‖ STREAKY AND BROWN, BUT SLEEK ‖

Greater roadrunners are sizable birds—about two feet long from the tip of the beak to the tip of the tail. They are buff colored with heavy brown streaks, and they sport shaggy, blue-black crests. Their long iridescent tails, which show colors of blue and green, have large white spots. Colorful patches of bare skin in hues of orange, white, and sky blue surround the eyes. The purpose of this multi-colored area is not well understood, but it may aid in sexual or individual recognition. The colored skin is sometimes obscured by feathers and is often difficult to see. Large, wild eyes give the bird a defiant, startled look. Their pale blue legs are strong and adapted for running.

The male and female differ only slightly in appearance. The roadrunner's shape and the color of its feathers blend well with its habitat, making it virtually invisible when hiding in a tree or bush.

Flapping its wings and leaping about, this roadrunner hopes to stir up an insect or two.

LIVELY, COLORFUL NAMES

Many common names have been applied to the roadrunner—in fact, probably more names than for any other bird. The scientific name for the greater roadrunner may be the least flashy of them all. *Geococcyx californianus* comes from the Greek *geo,* meaning "earth," and *kokkyks,* meaning "cuckoo." *Californianus* refers to the state of California, one area of the roadrunner's range, so this bird is a "California earth cuckoo." The birds were originally dubbed roadrunners because they were observed running down roadways ahead of horse-drawn vehicles.

One of the bird's most evocative names is "snake killer," a reference to an old cowpoke tale in which the bird was purported to be a shrewd antagonist of rattlesnakes. Other nicknames include "lizard bird," undoubtedly originating from the birds' propensity for eating lizards. In Spanish, greater roadrunner is known as *correcaminos norteño* and also as *correo del camino,* which translates literally as "runner of the road." In many parts of Mexico, the bird is referred to as *paisano,* meaning "compatriot" or "fellow countryman." In Mexico's northern state of Sonora, it is often called *churea,* a name thought to represent one of the sounds the bird makes.

Dance of death: roadrunners occasionally take on large rattlesnakes.

It has been called "chaparral cock" or "chaparral bird" in California because of its affinity for living in arid brushlands known as chaparral. The bird's impish, devil-may-care demeanor may have inspired the nickname "cock of the desert." In yet another reference to its primary habitat, the name "desert clown" probably came from

observations of the strange antics of these chiefly desert-dwelling birds. The name "ground cuckoo" aptly describes what the bird really is: a terrestrial member of the cuckoo family.

The sheer number of nicknames for this bird reveals that the roadrunner has attracted a lot of attention and been noticed by many people over the years.

WHY IS IT GREATER?

A close relative of the greater roadrunner is the lesser roadrunner, known in Spanish as *correcaminos tropical.* Found in arid scrub and farmlands from western Mexico south to Nicaragua, the lesser roadrunner is smaller, only about seventeen to twenty inches long. Differentiating the two species in the field can be difficult. They are very similar in appearance, although the lesser roadrunner has less streaking on its neck and chest.

HABITAT AND RANGE

Generally warm-weather fans, roadrunners enjoy regions with lots of sunshine and low humidity. Within the extensive range that they inhabit year-round, habitat can vary quite a bit. They favor arid

With tail and wings fanned, the bird carefully circles the snake …

regions with cactus and mesquites, but they also seem to be at home among the piñon pines and junipers of mountain foothills. Roadrunners are most common in the Sonoran and Chihuahuan Deserts of northern Mexico, southeastern California, southern Arizona, southern New Mexico, and western Texas. In California their range extends northward into dry central valleys and even reaches the San Francisco Bay area. Away from the deserts that form the heart of their range, these adaptable birds may be found north and east to Colorado, Oklahoma, Louisiana, Arkansas, southern Kansas, and even the Ozarks of Missouri. A series of cold winters at the edge of their range can bring about population declines, as prolonged snow cover cuts down on the availability of food.

LEGENDS AND FOLKLORE

Legends and tall tales about roadrunners abound. One of the best known is a cowboy tale in which the roadrunner was purported to be a clever conqueror of rattlesnakes. The story suggests that the bird was capable of trapping a sleeping rattlesnake by encircling it with joints of spiny, round-stemmed cactus—presumably cholla. After completing a kind of makeshift fence or corral, the bird

… but sometimes the best ones get away.

would wake up the snake by dropping cactus joints on it. When the snake attempted to escape the "corral," it would fatally injure itself on the cactus spines and would then be eaten by the roadrunner.

Some Native American societies attributed supernatural powers to the roadrunner and called it Medicine Bird, War Bird, or Snake Eater. In Pueblo culture, a secure afterlife could be guaranteed if people placed X-shaped roadrunner tracks around the house of a deceased individual. Because two toes point forward and two backward, it was difficult to determine which direction the bird was headed. Evil spirits would be misled by this and confused as to the direction taken by the departed soul. Another legend held that if the soles and palms of people attending funerals were marked with an "X," the mark of the roadrunner's feet, it would keep the dead from following them. Some tribes of the Great Plains placed roadrunner feathers and skins over lodge doors to generate good luck and to baffle evil spirits.

Among Native Americans, roadrunners have traditionally symbolized courage, strength, and endurance. Some native peoples hunted and ate these birds in the hope of acquiring some of their traits. The Tarahumara of Mexico's Sierra Madre region, swift

Scanning for prey.

runners in their own right, believed that if they caught and ate roadrunners, they would be endowed with great speed and endurance. Hopi people tied roadrunner feathers to the tails of their horses in the hope of instilling speed in their stallions and mares. Because the birds were observed fighting and often capturing rattlesnakes, they were regarded as symbols of bravery.

In some areas of Mexico, eating the flesh of roadrunners was believed to cure itches and boils, purify the blood, and even stimulate the growth of flowers! Other cultures believed that roadrunners delivered babies, paralleling the popular notion elsewhere that this was the province of another large and strange-looking bird, the stork. Contrary to the idea that the X-shaped footprints of roadrunners would create directional confusion, some early frontier dwellers actually believed the birds would lead a lost person to a trail, thereby saving them from a long, slow death in the desert.

THE ROADRUNNER AND THE COYOTE

With episode titles such as "Highway Runnery," "To Beep or Not to Beep," and "Beep Prepared," a long-running Warner Brothers cartoon series featured the roadrunner and another Southwestern

A rare partially albino roadrunner.

character, Wile E. Coyote. Road Runner, loosely based on the real bird, was flightless and was continually being chased down the highways of the Southwest by a hungry coyote who thought the bird would make a tasty meal. Wile E. never catches the roadrunner, even though the coyote obtains a number of complex and harebrained devices from a mail-order catalog in attempts to destroy the bird. The coyote's plans usually backfire, and he finds himself singed, flattened, or befuddled at the bottom of a ravine—generally more humiliated than actually harmed by his failures. These cartoons had no dialogue other than the occasional "beep beep" of the roadrunner, although plenty of deafening sound effects were produced by Wile E.'s crazy experiments and shenanigans.

IT'S A CAR

One tribute to the roadrunner's speed was the creation of the Plymouth Roadrunner in 1968. The car, based on the Looney Tunes cartoon, included a horn that blasted—guess what?—"beep beep!" The steering wheel sported an illustration of a roadrunner, as did the air cleaner. In 1970 a second automobile called the

Plymouth Superbird was released and went one step further: a grand roadrunner wearing a helmet adorned the car's large rear spoiler.

BORN TO RUN

This bird that looks like something out of Jurassic Park seems ungainly until it begins to move. Suddenly it becomes a streamlined speed machine, holding its head and wings parallel to the ground, swinging its long tail, and using it as a rudder as it changes direction.

With a sleek body and strong legs built for speed, it can maintain running clips of up to fifteen miles per hour over considerable distances in pursuit of lizards, insects, or other prey. Roadrunners support their weight alternately on one leg and then the other, and they generally prefer to ramble along roads, paths, or dry streambeds, favoring open areas for easier walking and running.

Roadrunners are seemingly loath to fly, but when pursued, these ground-dwelling creatures may fly into a tree or shrub to hide. They may also fly off a road if a car gets too close. Flying is usually restricted to gliding from a high perch or a nest site.

LIZARDS AND MORE FOR LUNCH

Roadrunners have appetites to match their size and will eat just about anything that comes their way. Any small creature is fair game, from grasshoppers to rodents to small toads to scorpions to rattlesnakes. Animal foods make up about 90 percent of their diet, and roadrunners rely heavily on insects year-round. Lizards and grasshoppers seem to be their favorite delicacies, although primary food items tend to change with the seasons. Insects, more easily captured than reptiles, are abundantly available during the summer

months. Lizards, snakes, and mice are captured mainly during the breeding season and provide nutritious protein for the growing young. During the winter months, when cold temperatures reduce the activity of insects, spiders, and reptiles, roadrunners feed chiefly on small birds, seeds, and fruits. They sometimes dine on cactus fruits, knocking the spiny treats to the ground and then smacking them around repeatedly in order to break off the spines.

Roadrunners also devour the eggs and young of many species of birds and other animals. Inexperienced young are probably ambushed shortly after they have left the care of their parents. Young bats that have fallen from the ceilings of caves or have somehow injured themselves are also fair game. Even adult birds may be captured. Small mammals make fine meals. Mice, gophers, ground squirrels, rabbits, and voles may all be caught and eaten by these predatory cuckoos.

MIGHTY HUNTERS

Almost more interesting than what they eat is how roadrunners conquer their prey. Crafty hunters, they search for food on the ground in open areas, but they can leap quickly upward to pick off a grasshopper or small bird from a shrub or tree. As they forage along the desert floor, they walk and run, periodically pausing to visually scan for things to eat. Sometimes they flush insects or other creatures from the ground simply while moving about. At other times they make more of an effort by leaping into the air and flapping their wings, stirring up whatever insects are in the immediate vicinity.

A male mounts a female with a food "gift" in his bill.

Roadrunners frequently catch smaller birds at feeders and bird-houses—even fast-flying hummingbirds. The roadrunner may stake out a hummingbird feeder and sit in wait. When the hummer flies in, the roadrunner leaps four to six feet off the ground to snag the tiny creature. Low-flying bats and aerial birds such as white-throated swifts may be knocked to the ground with a similar sudden upward leap.

Depending on the type of prey, roadrunners proceed in different ways. After seizing small birds in their heavy bills, they pluck the feathers before feasting. They seize scorpions by the tail, and small mammals such as mice are killed by striking a blow to the base of the animal's skull. When capturing larger prey such as lizards or young ground squirrels, the roadrunner strikes them against a rock or the ground, slamming them up to twenty times per minute. The larger the prey, the greater number of times it is beaten. The road-runner may take fifteen minutes or more to beat its prey into sub-mission. This repeated beating breaks down the skeleton of the prey, making it longer and narrower, and thus easier to swallow.

To protect the eyes during aggressive maneuvers, a thin, trans-parent membrane closes over the roadrunner's eyeballs during an

Open wide!

attack. This third "eyelid," called a nictating membrane, acts somewhat like goggles. Protecting the bird's eyes, it also keeps them from drying out.

Roadrunners prefer to capture small, defenseless lizards such as whiptails, but they will also take large, armored species such as horned lizards. Horned lizards, despite their spiky horns, are seized, grasped, and swallowed head first. The bird orients the lizard's body so that the horns point away from the bird's heart and lungs. In this manner the lizard passes through the bird's expanded throat and esophagus, and damage to vital organs is avoided.

The "snake killer" favors small snakes such as garter or hognosed snakes but will challenge a large rattlesnake on occasion. Two birds may cooperate in an attack, circling and waiting for the opportunity to grasp the back of the snake's neck with their heavy bills. Agile and quick, the roadrunners avoid snake strikes by leaping into the air or dodging quickly backward. If a bird succeeds in seizing the snake's head, it tosses it into the air. When the stunned reptile lands on the ground, the bird grasps it in its beak and beats it into submission. The birds do not appear to suffer any ill effects from eating venomous species. Roadrunners are

Roadrunners prefer small, nonvenomous snakes to large rattlesnakes.

not always successful in conquering large snakes and will eventually back off if they seem to be losing the battle.

COPING WITH HEAT AND COLD

Roadrunners have evolved a number of physiological and behavioral adaptations for surviving in both hot and cold conditions. They have the remarkable ability to conserve energy by controlling their own body temperatures. In cold weather, roadrunners seek out windless locations and sunbathe by orienting their backs to the sun. They raise their back feathers, exposing the black skin of the spinal area, which acts as a solar panel, warming the entire body. Even nestlings have black skin capable of absorbing the sun's rays. During icy winter months, roadrunners economize their energy expenditures by hunting only during more favorable weather conditions. On cold nights, they may roost in dense trees that protect them from the wind. Occasionally they may sleep in an abandoned nest. In extremely severe weather, the birds may travel to the base of a cliff to seek out shelter and food among the rocks. Birds often fluff out their feathers when standing, walking, or running in order to insulate their bodies and reduce heat loss.

Birds preen to clean feathers and remove parasites.

In hot weather, roadrunners give off excess heat by evaporative water loss through both their skin and their respiratory systems. In a mechanism called "gular flutter," the bird pants and droops its wings, holding them away from its body, to allow air to flow through. Even five-day-old nestlings can maintain internal body temperature through gular fluttering. Restricting most of their activity to early morning and late afternoon also enables road-runners to conserve energy. The birds often retreat to the shade in midday and compress their feathers to retain less heat. They may also gape into a strong wind, letting the air run over their damp mouth parts. This acts like evaporative cooling and cools their bodies from within.

Roadrunners seem to obtain plenty of moisture from their food. However, if water is available, they drink copiously, holding their bills slightly open and parallel to the surface of the water. They do not normally bathe in water, but they relish dust bathing. Squatting on their bellies, they shuffle and flutter their wings to force dust through their feathers. Dust bathing may help maintain their feathers and also dislodges mites, fleas, and other parasites.

In cool weather, black feathers and dark skin help absorb the sun's warmth.

COOING AND WHINING

Neither "beep beep" nor dulcet tones are part of the roadrunner's vocal repertoire. Although generally silent, these birds do have an assortment of calls associated with different behaviors. These include a soft descending cooing, a growl, a whine, a whirr, and even a bark. And then there's a non-vocal bill clacking. What is the meaning of all these curious sounds produced by this peculiar bird?

The sweet-sounding coo is most frequently heard. In the spring, males often deliver a downward slurring *coo-coo-coo-coo-cooo* from the top of a tree or fencepost, or from an exposed rock, beginning at sunrise. Cooing may continue for several hours without the bird moving or changing its position. With each *coo,* the male raises its head slightly. This call denotes both territoriality and courtship.

During courting, single *coo* notes are given by both female and male birds, along with whirring and whining. Whirring, often interspersed with soft, mechanical "putting" sounds, is often made by males during courtship: *putt putt putt putt whirrr putt putt putt putt whirr.* A single long whine may be produced by either sex. Females often whine when at the nest site, and they also sometimes make a series of rapid barking sounds similar to the yips of coyotes.

BILL CLACKING

Another distinctive sound made by roadrunners adds yet another element to their mystique. By snapping the upper and lower portions of their bills together, they produce a rapid drumming sound, sometimes likened to the sound of castanets. This is accompanied by a vocal whine that originates in the bird's syrinx, or voice box.

Both sexes may engage in bill clacking in almost any season, but you will hear it most frequently during the nesting season. Birds stand with their ragged crests either partially or fully raised and drum the upper and lower portions of the bill together. Bill clacking is thought to help mates locate one another over long distances and may also serve as a warning signal if danger is perceived. For the alert birdwatcher, this distinctive sound is often the first clue that there is a roadrunner hiding in the brush nearby.

COURTSHIP

Roadrunners are generally monogamous, maintaining long-term pair bonds. Male and female defend a fairly large territory together, and each spring and summer they renew their vows through a series of vigorous courtship displays.

How could a female resist this?

They search for food together, usually several yards apart, staying in touch with regular bill clacking. Preliminary courtship displays include a spirited ground chase, which lasts for several hours, although both birds stop frequently to rest between turns pursuing each other. Their darts and dashes are sometimes interspersed with

low gliding flights. The pursuing bird lunges forward at the other with its wings and tail raised and fanned. In a less energetic, but possibly more romantic, strategy, the male may give a *coo* call from an elevated perch. The male may also approach the female with a "gift" (either food or nesting material), then spring into the air and hover above the female. Either sex may approach its mate carrying a stick in its bill, dropping the stick in front of the other bird or transferring it to the other bird's bill.

Males perform a prancing display, in which they run from the female with their wings and tail raised, then lower their wings, bringing them close to the body with a distinctive popping sound. Then the male uses its long, expressive tail, wagging it horizontally as it bows and slowly lifts its head. All the while the bird's crest is erect and the colorful patch of bare skin behind the eye is exposed. While the male's tail wags, the female responds with her tail, flicking it rapidly in a vertical plane.

NESTING

Males and females generally mate near the prospective nest site, usually located in a small tree or bush in an area without a lot of

Males and females have similar coloring and patches near the eyes.

other vegetation. Since open areas are needed for their energetic and elaborate courtship displays, extensive tracts of woody vegetation are less desirable.

Both male and female make frequent trips to the prospective nest site to determine if it is suitable. Overhanging leaves and branches are necessary for producing the dappled light that helps conceal the nest and nestlings. Nests are often situated near dry washes or livestock paths, allowing for easier access during nest construction and care of the young.

Nests are normally placed in thorny bushes, small trees, or in cacti about three to ten feet above the ground. Cholla cacti and hackberry, mesquite, and palo verde trees are favorites. In less arid regions, roadrunners will establish nest sites in juniper, elm, oak, and willow trees. The nests are well concealed, placed near the center of the plant in a crotch of a branch or resting on a horizontal bough. Occasionally a pair will nest in an unusual location such as in an opening on a cliff face, on an old tractor, or in some other piece of neglected farm machinery.

The nest is a shallow, compact platform of thorny sticks loosely laid together, often lined with finer materials such as grass, leaves,

Young birds hatch with their eyes closed.

and feathers. Sometimes a snakeskin will be added to the collection. Adult birds enter the nest from the ground by clambering from limb to limb with their clawed feet. When leaving the nest, they generally extend their wings and glide to the ground. Females do most of the nest building, but males collect and carry twigs and other nesting material to the site. If the male seems to be abandoning his role as twig provider, the female signals him with a whiney call. This seems to bring the male back to the task at hand— a renewed gathering of twigs.

Female roadrunners lay anywhere from three to six eggs. The eggs, covered with a chalky yellowish film, are laid one by one, approximately every other day. Incubation begins with the first egg laid, resulting in widely spaced hatching times. As a result, the young in any one nest may be of different sizes and stages of development.

The parents take turns sitting on the eggs, incubating almost continuously for about twenty days. Females tend to incubate for longer periods during the day, and the males incubate mostly at night. Even after the eggs hatch, the diligent adults do not leave the nest unattended; one parent patiently waits until the other arrives to relieve it before taking off in search of yet more food for the hungry young. The newly hatched chicks are fed insects, but as they grow, the parents provide crushed lizards and small snakes, which provide protein as well as moisture.

NEW GENERATIONS

Roadrunners are altricial (pronounced al-TRISH-al), from the Latin *altrix,* meaning nurse or wet nurse. Altricial birds hatch in a helpless state, usually with their eyes closed. Unable to leave the nest for a few weeks, they are completely dependent upon their parents for food and care.

By about six days of age, nestlings can produce buzzy notes and hissing sounds. The young are ready to leave the nest in about fourteen to twenty-five days. Shy and timid at first, they may perch in the nest tree for a day or so. Each day, the parents coax the young birds farther and farther away from the nest site, luring them with food and muffled, purring calls. Once the young leave the nest tree or shrub, they remain in the general vicinity for several days, mostly hiding in vegetation. At sixteen days of age, the young are able to clack their bills, bob their tails, and raise the feathers of their crests. At about three weeks of age, they are capable of catching their own food.

Grasshoppers are a favorite delicacy.

For the most part, roadrunners produce only one brood per year, but occasionally a pair will bring off a second clutch following the summer rainy season. If predators take eggs or young from a nest, the adult pair will often make a second attempt at nesting. Depending on the timing, some clutches may face food shortages, since the numbers of active grasshoppers and lizards decline during the fall months.

Roadrunners have a reputation for being somewhat barbaric with their young. Nestlings that act lethargic and do not beg for food may be thrown up into the air and swallowed whole by the parents or fed to stronger siblings. The larger, more developed chicks in a clutch may chuck their younger siblings out of the nest. Adult birds also have been known to eat their young during severe food shortages.

ENEMIES AND DEFENSE

Roadrunners are thought to be fairly long-lived, but information on their lifespan is not well documented. Adult birds are usually quick enough to evade ground-dwelling predators; avian predators, however, pose a different problem. Surprising the victim from above, hawks may swoop down rapidly to seize an unsuspecting bird. Red-tailed and Cooper's hawks use the element of surprise to ambush roadrunners, and crows and ravens have also been known to attack them. Animals such as coyotes, raccoons, skunks, and bobcats feast upon roadrunner eggs and nestlings. Some types of snakes also eat the eggs and young: rat snakes, coachwhips, and bullsnakes are common culprits.

The remains of a raided nest often reveal what type of predator has been at work. Mammals are able to reach only low-lying nests located at the edge of a shrub or tree. As they plunder, they often cause damage to the actual nest structure, and hair and eggshells are sometimes left in the vicinity. Predators such as snakes are better able to penetrate dense thorn cover that surrounds nests and may swallow the entire contents of the nest, leaving no trace behind.

Of course, roadrunners are not defenseless. If attacked from above by a predator such as a hawk, they may dodge, flash their wings, and spread their expressive tails. In order to lure predators away from the nest site, adults often use distraction techniques, feigning injury to their wings or acting as if they have a broken leg. Scrambling to the ground and falling over on their sides, they drag

themselves away from the nest area in full view of the predator, with wings held closed and at their sides. They may flop around and repeat this behavior until the predator has been lured away and the threat has passed.

A roadrunner swallows a horned lizard head first.

OF ROADRUNNERS AND HUMANS

In the past roadrunners were persecuted because they were believed to be responsible for eating the eggs and chicks of quail, a popular game bird. Federal and state bounties, called "chaparral drives" (a reference to the nickname "chaparral bird"), were imposed in the

Roadrunners can take to the air when necessary.

early twentieth century in an attempt to rescue what was thought to be a declining quail population. Rumors about quail predation may have originated from observations of roadrunners tailing groups of quail. Roadrunners will in fact closely follow other animals—and

Preening in some hard-to-reach places.

farm plows as well—in order to gobble down the insects that are flushed from the ground by the movement. These are meals too easy to pass up. Some studies of the diets of roadrunners reveal that quail are rarely consumed and point out that roadrunners are actually quite useful in controlling crop and household pests. Despite the valuable service they offer in terms of pest control, roadrunners continue to be shot illegally. And many lose their lives to cars or trucks, particularly when crossing highways.

Roadrunner populations seem to be most affected by urbanization, which limits the availability and numbers of large insects and small animals. Non-native, exotic plants associated with urban landscapes may be another factor, as the birds find them unsuitable for nesting. Numbers are also affected by household pets and feral animals, as well as by pedestrian and vehicular traffic. The birds continue to nest in more open suburban areas where they can find clumps of native vegetation appropriate for nesting. Despite the persistence of illegal hunting and a drop-off in numbers in some areas, roadrunners do not seem to face serious declines in population, and they continue to expand their range both eastward and northward.

On a chilly morning, fluffed feathers create more insulation.

AN APACHE LEGEND

According to one Apache tale, different types of birds got together and discussed the fact that other animals seemed to have leaders, whereas they did not. So they began to contemplate who among their ranks would make a good leader. Their first thought was the oriole because of its beautiful colors. But despite its attractive plumage, it wasn't a very vocal bird, so they felt it might not speak well as their leader. The next idea was the mockingbird. Too talkative, they decided, and besides that, it often spoke poorly and mocked things. The blue jay was proposed, but the group decided that it also talked too much, was stubborn, and had a habit of bragging. Finally, they thought of the roadrunner. It would be fast for running to meetings, and it talked well. Because of these attributes, the birds decided that the roadrunner would make a good chieftain. And so it became the leader of all birds.

SUGGESTED READING

Kaufman, Kenn. *Lives of North American Birds.* Boston,
Massachusetts: Houghton Mifflin Co., 1996.

Kaufman, Lynn Hassler. *Birds of the American Southwest.* Tucson,
Arizona: Rio Nuevo Publishers, 2000.

Meinzer, Wyman. *The Roadrunner.* Lubbock, Texas: Texas Tech
University Press, 1993.

PHOTOGRAPHY © AS FOLLOWS